I0654287

MYSTIC BOXING COMMISSION

®

SPARRING
★ ★ ★ ALL-STARS
SERIES

Word Troubadours

ELLYN MAYBE & PJ SWIFT

SPARRING ALL-STARS SERIES

★ ★ ★ ★

ELLYN MAYBE, a Southern California based poet, United States Artist nominee, is the author of numerous books, and is widely anthologized. She also has two highly acclaimed poetry/music albums, *Rodeo for the Sheepish* (Hen House Studios) and *Skywriting with Glitter* (ellyn & robbie).

Once upon a time, **PJ SWIFT** embarked on a pursuit of creating a story, a lyric or an anecdote a day... a thousand and one nights have come and gone (now over 2,222 and counting) and PJ Swift has not emerged since...each piece an individual entity existing in its own poetic realm.

WORD TROUBADOURS

by PJ SWIFT and ELLYN MAYBE

Published by:

ISBN: 979-8-9905623-8-7
Publisher: Mystic Boxing Commission
Copyright © 2025 PJ Swift and Ellyn Maybe

Front cover art: "Horse Pipe and Red Flower"
by Joan Miro (oil painting 1920)
Back cover art: "The Poet" by Ángel Zárraga

Artwork "The Poet" by Ángel Zárraga

TABLE OF CONTENTS

TITLE   **PAGE**

CINEMA DANCE

Cinema plus dance.
Invocation, fezzes, hot chocolate.
UNESCO barrier reefs, unseen Griffin.
Deer crossed with horse, a hybrid…just like us.
We come from all over the Globe,
    shaken like a snow crusted city in a Medieval handstand.
We gleefully take towns by storm with our
    Merry Prankster bus selves.
Three and a half days of cameras, ping pong and pivo.
We compose a shot list from confetti.
We are part speed of light.
Jules and Jim at midnight.
We resist the temptation to crawl into the world
    and pull our psyches over our heads.
In a universe where dance ruled, we'd see fewer body bags.
We are Cinemascope.
Chromakey with chromosomes.
We are taking back the ozone layer that tries to stomp
    artists out and put them in tiny flowery picket places.
We go where others have gone and others will go.
Van Gogh and Truffaut danced once.
It's an everlasting dance.
We are one tin can line away from the sky.
We need our exuberance more than our math.
We need to let our lights shine.
Cinema Dance is the longest magic hour.
Let us leave a bread trail, our bread crumbs are evident.
Feeding the soul is society's true hunger.
Dobre Chut!!!

---ellyn maybe

THE TWO TINY GRAINS OF MARBLE

They were two tiny grains of marble, snugly packed together for millions of years. Already they were quite noble within the mineral world. Not diamonds, of course, but marble was still high-class among all the rocks and stones and sand and dirt out there. And then suddenly, to much excitement, the two grains were part of a slab extracted for the services of a great renaissance sculpture. Without exaggeration, this was a once in a million-year event. The skilled sculptor tried his hand at the slab but finding the marbles' qualities not suited to his talents, cast it aside. The slab and its two closely snug grains lay dormant for over a decade (which was no time at all for marble) when an even more miraculous event transpired. The great Michelangelo took possession of the marble, focusing his talent, love, and passion into transforming this slab into a transcendent work of art. With skill and care, he devoted himself to chipping, chiseling, and carving the slab with his full divine affection. Before the great artist was finished, the power of this monumental work was evident, and even the slab of marble itself, down to each and every one of its individual particles, became imbued with essential vitality as if touched by the hand of God. Now, the masterpiece is virtually finished. The work, Michelangelo's Pieta, would live with a permanence and essence beyond the marble's elementary millions of years. All that was left was one final scrape of the master to render this statue its eternal state. And with that fine movement, the two grains, born from crystals millions of years ago, so tightly bound since the beginning of time were separated, released from their embrace. One remained, forever an integral part of Pieta, the other discarded, the final grain relegated to a pile of dust. They were companions no more, their destinies radically transformed.

The original grain remains a part of the Pieta today. They are one and the same, the material essential to the spirit. But this story also has a happy ending for the other grain that had been swept aside. An assistant cleaned the studio floor and collected the powder that included the errant grain. That powder was collected and used as an ingredient for plaster. Plaster that the master later used for a fresco in another great work -- the ceiling of the Sistine Chapel. There as God reaches out to Adam granting the gift of eternal life, on the very, farthest tip of his finger, is that other grain of marble. Cast aside no more.
Blessed by the breath of art.

---pj swift

PICASSO

I found a year that likes my body
1921
girl sitting on a rock
Picasso painted a woman
with my thighs

walking around the museum
it hit me how Rubenesque
is not just some word
for someone who likes corned beef

there I was
naked on the edge of something
overlooking water
or was it salt

it was weird
nobody was screaming fat chick at the frame
nobody was making grieving sounds
but the girl in the painting looked sad
as though she knew
new eras were smudging
a forced liposuction
with rough acrylic

the caption said
girl sitting on rock

not woman who uses food to help cope
for the lack of empathy in her sphere

not the gyms are closed and there are
better muscles to develop

not girl one calorie away
from suicide

just flesh on a rock

her eyes dripping
question marks onto
girl looking into a mirror

the vibrancy
the need to chew the ice cubism
till the teeth bleed
the colors so deep
they look wet

the museum guards
watch me tentatively
I lean into the painting
I veer to the outside
to find out what Picasso
called each work

I like titles
their vocabulary of oil
the girl on the rock
whispered to me

go girl

I love museums
call me old fashioned
but I like face to face
conversations.

---ellyn maybe

THAT LITTLE SONG

Everyone knew that song. Nobody considered it their favorite. But they kind of liked it and accepted it. A sweet, silly, harmless little tune. It stayed around for a while and made its comeback decades later.

It survived because all those little moments that people shared and remembered all that variety of emotion, latched onto that song. That song was an emotional bank. It stored what otherwise would have disappeared forever -- the emotional substance of so many lives.

That song was like currency. Not particularly distinguishable or valuable in itself, but it was a denomination of worth.

And so the song was played, and sung and remembered, gaining value over the years. And far into the future, serving as a testament that we were here.

---pj swift

I HEARD WHAT SOUNDED LIKE A SONG

It sounded like la.
I started to hum with the knowing melody.
Suddenly the voice got louder
   and it didn't sound like la anymore.
The voice said live.

I looked around and there was Joan of Arc.
She said Leonard Cohen got me right.
Music is the highest calling.
She said live.

I know it's not easy being a woman who knows the
   difference between Gene Kelly and Gene Krupa,
   Miles Davis and Miles Traveled.
I know how men make women wear armor of all kinds.

It's natural to think of blowing out your candles.
When you read Tennessee Williams,
   many things go through one's mind.

It's hard to watch angels go to bed with wings and
   in the morning, it's ash.

Dreyer got it right.
The soul is in the eyes.
Close-up.

She said I'm a trick candle.
They think they extinguished me, but I never completely go out.
Live.

My body is not my soul. Of course not.
I know martyrs from all times and seasons.

We play mahjong in Heaven, we read comic books.
We are not 24/7 serious.
That's what really scared them.

Every them through history is afraid of what's brimming and
   can't be controlled.
When she spoke, smoke came from her mouth like the grate of a
   Manhattan street.
Like a dragon.

She nodded it's my DNA now.
My descendants, wherever they may be,
    they will recognize each other.

Of course we can tell the chain smokers from the saints.
We are not naive.
Everyone wants a puff of immortality without having to die.
Death is a passing fancy.

Still for one glittering moment, I wanted a knight in shining
    armor to rescue me.
Like Guinevere and Lancelot.
But I was King Arthur.

My hands were tied.
I assure you, I miss the grass I used to walk on barefoot.
My feet were so much dust so quickly.

I was a girl who played hopscotch.
I was a girl who picked berries and had little girl crushes.
I was a little girl.

Live hung in the air like the notes you hear after the
    opera is over.
The reverberations last forever.

--- ellyn maybe

WAR OF THE ARTS

It started with the wailing. The adversaries sent multiple divisions of singers to the front who launched a barrage of songs. Ballads, blues, country, rock, and opera, from duets to full scale choirs.

For a moment all was silent and still.

Then hundreds of planes flew overhead dropping thousands of tiny parachutes, each carrying a unique and original poem. Unfolding the tiny pieces of paper to read the thousands of poems overwhelmed the sensitive feelings of the citizenry and their forces. They were virtually incapacitated.

And then came the tap dancers, the contortionists, mimes, and jugglers, creating merry bedlam as they frolicked merrily throughout the lands for several days and several nights. When their revelry was finally over, the sprayers came in marking all the territory that had been conquered by art.

---pj swift

BEING AN ARTIST

Being an artist
means the recession will always be there
and has always been here
while you sit not writing screenplays
not taking meetings
just writing love letters to Van Gogh's beard
not wearing a watch
not caring who's on the cover of *People* magazine

Being an artist
means you might sleep awfully late
you might choose totally different things
as the four major food groups

Being an artist
might mean you feel depressed and make others feel
distressed when they are near you

Being an artist
means you've probably memorized the aisles at the 99 cents store
you probably have a $12 service charge each month for low funds in
your checking account

Being an artist
means you don't feel you have the right to remain silent

Being an artist
might make people think you're on drugs

Being an artist
means people think your closet is full of turtlenecks and mood rings
people assume you play harmonica
people assume you know all the words to every song
released in the 1960's

Being an artist
means you do

Being an artist
means serenity, intensity, sometimes simultaneously

Being an artist
means you have the power of civil disobedience on the tip of your tongue

Artwork by Vincent van Gogh - "Self-Portrait"

Being an artist
means shrinking tie-dyed tee-shirts cause you were thinking about a poem
and didn't notice the washer was on hot water

Being an artist
is an active verb
a noun
a consonant
an adjective in a world full of chaotic life sentences

Being an artist is not necessarily a choice

---ellyn maybe

Art "Archaeopteyx" by Ernest Seton Thompson

THE FIRST RHYME

Somewhere deep in prehistoric days, the first bird appeared (indeed, upon hatching from an egg). Strutting and stretching its wings, this very young (but ancient) bird opened its beak, releasing its first sound -- an awkward, primal squeak -- into a raw and empty world.

Shortly later a similar sound returned to the bird. He hopped about excitedly. He was not alone in this world. Perhaps he had a friend. The little bird squeaked again. The sound returned. Again, and again.
Squeak squeak. Squeak squeak.
But the sounds were not from another bird. This was his own echo. Echoes reverberating his own voice. Squeaks that rhythmically replicated his original cries.

And so, the bird discovered rhyme. Not fully alone in the world, he had his rhyme and poetry to keep him company, waiting until one day the whole sky would sing.

Squeak squeak squeak and so many other melodious and impassioned sounds....

---pj swift

SOMEWHERE IN THE SKY

What if every moment you feel something happening.
Someone scattering daisies and someone throwing ash.
What if you feel the bones of history in the ache
    of the land.
What if you wake up and your head is a map in
    a million different languages.
What if you are able to eat musical notes for breakfast
    and symphonies for snacks.
What if documentaries are written in your eyelids
    like rain.
What if you listen to everything written with a
    crescendo of breath.
What if everything blended Technicolor wonder, but
    only for an hour.
Would you wake up early or stay up all night in order
    to find it?
What if your sky shimmered with glitter.
What if your hemisphere drizzled with doom.
A thesaurus of moments, human in nature.
Would you live in the clouds or relish Earth's hue.
Perhaps life is a multiple choice question my friend.
The answer's in a circle dance with no beginning or end.

---ellyn maybe

CREATION OF MYTHS

Elon Musk never did pay
nor commission this poem
nor provide inspiration
(ok, not totally fair -- there is something
in the air: a musk [ha!]
peculiar and loathsome)

still words require
(even those of omission)
reasons to soar, sparks of cognition
idling, senselessly
on our grand avenue of life
an era whose burdens
have granted no choice

destiny demands (ergo, a titan commands!)
a masterly, wrought-out epic
an ode to our crimes
Hidden spirits, bruised souls,
pause and insist
such usurpation: must it persist?
please, pleas arise before creation of myths

who owns our lives and who owns our age
who owns our words and who owns our rage
who makes the melody and who sets the meter
Peter pays Paul
but who must pay Peter?

every bright dawn spawns words
that we rue
each definition cannot be untrue

that epic will rise, as sure as our day
can these words absorb power
from sharp burning rays?

our meager testament has no aim to exalt
nor fascinate, marvel, bedevil – find fault

no muddling the score
with origin stories
no appeasement of pains
in pursuit of false glory

we inhabit our time
we did not ask to exist
we flounder, we wonder
if we live -- we resist

---pj swift

2016: THE YEAR THE 20TH CENTURY FINALLY DIED

The year so many musicians died and the year
    Freedom seemed to be moving underground
Caskets filled the air.
We live in times of turmoil, clocks beating quicker and quicker.
Middle age seems old.
Seniors seem timeless.

There's a lethargy in the way people move .
There's a liturgy on the tip of our tongues.
There's something in the morning cereal.
It looks like newsprint.
There's something in the evening news.
It seems like farce.
As though this couldn't be real.

This over the top peek into tragedy's eyelid.
This shiver that lives in our psyche like snow.
We ski into another winter.
The world is on a ski lift.
Cocoa is leaving its face around a cup.
We stir and it's January.
We stir and it's the 20th Century.
We stir and it looks like it's black and white newsreels.
History tries to repeat itself as the people in power like sequels.
People wear the hero mask, the death mask, the face and the heart.
People make choices. The stores sell everything.

One of the strongest songs from Rodgers and Hammerstein,
You've Got to Be Carefully Taught,
Prejudging is the name of the game so many household's play.
Play Rummikub instead.
Play solitaire, don't be influenced by peers.
One minute to midnight but people don't know if the year
    will leave us dangling from some threshold.
History said, look at me with your eyes aflame.
Burn my pain in your memory.
Walk into the libraries and kiss all the spines.

The Earth is spinning whether people stay on it or not.
What if Earth falls in the forest and nobody is there to hear it.
The last person on Earth will carry a pencil.
That is why Earth has survived this long.

---ellyn maybe

IMAGINATIONS, UNFROZEN

Swift wanders through the alternate realities provided by his imagination. (He does not question what influences his vision. Is it original thought, highly derivative of imposed structures, or imitative of the outputs he has encountered reading and watching preceding, more intrepid imaginations?).

He comes to a pleasant street-side cafe, where an older writer sits comfortably at work. Swift asks what he is working on, and the writer happily tells him he is writing a story about a glorious city made of ice cream. Everything is fragrant, flavorful, colorful, and cool.

Swift wanders off and, in no time, is back again the next day. The writer is despondent. Everything has melted. The entire city is gone. Swift tries to reassure the writer that everything can freeze again. But the writer complains that it can't return. Everything is melted goo. If it freezes, it will become just frozen puddles with everything still blended together without form. Swift asks the writer if he can imagine a process in which the melted ice cream can freeze again and reconstitute itself in the glorious frozen city the man first described. But the writer says that is impossible. He had carefully and diligently carved and created the city of frozen ice cream. But he forgot to mind the power source, so all is gone. It is his fault. There is nothing to be done.

Except to start anew. Completely anew.

---pj swift

ELLYN MAYBE'S DREAM

Girl…poet belongs in 1960's...folksinger…very Nouvelle Wave
Guy…part Edward G. Robinson…loves noir…pulp novels…
secretly musicals
Gargoyle…smart, funny, nice and extremely hip to music

The first two characters live in a tiny Midwestern town where they meet at
Just Like Tom Thumb's Blues Café at the open mic hootenanny night.
The girl performs some Dylan poetry from *Tarantula* and the guy sings
Desolation Row.
Bob Dylan is a huge life raft in their metaphoric desert, so they quickly
decide to write a musical about the characters in Dylan's songs.

They love being different. At the very same time, it's something that's
caused emotional bruises and skinned knees since they were kids.
Loneliness, precociousness, chance.

They decide to play pin the tail with a map and whatever country, town, or
continent they land on, they'll go.
While blindfolded listening to spinning, whirling, dervish songs, she
suddenly reached with her thumbtack wand and decided their not so
simple twist of fate.

He says, hey doll, where for art we headed?
She says, smiling and jumping up and down, we're going to Prague.
He says, wow!

They are both ecstatic she picked some place further than Chattanooga or
Dallas or Alabama or even Alaska.
She was grateful she was wearing heels that day, so she propelled the
thumbtack into Central Europe.
In flats, she would have picked Michigan or some M place. She had that
knowledge.

She knew Allen Ginsberg had been the King of May in Prague. She knew he
had been kicked out too. That's what she wanted. To be Queen and then to
be returned to herself.

She related to Kafka, of course, like every Jewish outsider who grew up on
Woody Allen films and gefilte fish.
She felt she'd know Prague on sight like Salvador Dali some night got in
her eyes and the things she'd see…the melting Astronomical Clock, the
Vltava with its lions and circuses underwater.

She saw illuminated manuscripts on her tongue when she brushed her teeth. On every tooth she saw a saga, a hymn, something from some other time. She saw the library burning at Alexandria every night. She felt the books march into her like a squadron of drowned soldiers asking to be saved.

She reads all the time. Never sleeping. She was the one who would remember. The books traipsed into her room like she was some call girl. At all hours, she'd have Dostoyevsky showing up with a roulette wheel. She had Madame Bovary wet with oceans knocking in the middle of the night. She saw a room full of bugs as evidence that Kafka had slept there.

She saw the crazy ink, the melancholy topography of many scribes. Suddenly the girl woke up. She had a slightly sweaty forehead. She told the guy I had this vivid dream, but somehow, I forgot it. I was reading or was I being read to?

When they got to Prague, it was so beautiful. The theaters looked like cakes…gold icing, murals, horses, everything. She never knew there could be so many kinds of cobblestones.

She had tried to learn Czech before coming to Prague. The first word she learned was "slunce" meaning "sun." The language came intricate and quickly out of the speakers' mouths. Everywhere she went, she felt people were talking of philosophers, musicians, and alchemy. Many were only making a bit of small talk, but she imagined she was missing out, not knowing.

On the other hand, she had spent so many years in America knowing exactly what people were saying. This was not necessarily an advantage. All the words with rough edges, all the endless talk about reality TV, all the eternal chatter like contemplation was nefarious or something.

The Charles Bridge was beautiful, but she didn't feel compelled to linger there like others. It was the side street architecture she felt deep in her marrow. It wasn't just the various styles of architecture alone, but the sculpture, painting, sgraffito, ornamentation, and most of all the people in their stone state. They were their own Prague…a nation of gargoyles. At night you could hear their speeches, their music, their litany of witness.

Others looked like angels. Some held up balconies, their Verona, the lovely soliloquies of this magical and haunted city. Sometimes they held their bodies a certain way, practically leaning into eternity.

One day she was singing all kinds of songs as she walked in the night. She felt safe enough to enjoy the way past twilight hours on certain streets.

There she would sing and sing. *Tangled Up In Blue*, *Love Is A 4 Letter Word*, and *Adelaide's Lament*.

Suddenly someone said Bob Dylan, Joan Baez and Frank Loesser. She looked around and nobody seemed to be talking to her or even looking her way. But she looked up and smiling at her was a gargoyle wearing a t-shirt with a picture of *Starry Starry Night*.

He winked, "That's Van Gogh and a little bit Don McLean.
This was seriously unusual for anyone to get her references, let alone a gargoyle.
She sang more songs; he knew all the lyrics too.
It was as though he was waiting for her to come to Prague and walk down this street.
He looked more human than gargoyle like he had just jumped into the building for her benefit, but he looked like he had been restored.

He told her how he had once been a composer, a painter, a poet, a baker, but a few credits short to be a candlestick maker. He was one of the Renaissance people alive during the Renaissance who nobody remembers anymore. He was in Shakespeare's shadow. If not him, then somebody else. Shadows drove him crazy...now he cast his own.

She listened to his psychology unfold and told him that the guy she came with walked into a hospoda and walked out with a girlfriend and now he was history, so to speak, and here they had come all this way to write a musical about the characters in Bob Dylan's songs.

She started to ask him if he had any time.

She caught herself. He said, look, I don't want a pity gig just cause I've been on this building since 1348. I was here before this building was. The building is here because of me. I used to live in a tree, it can always be done, but sometimes this takes a toll after 100 years or so. Suddenly he started to talk about directors and playwrights and penguins and where the peanut butter and jelly sandwich was invented, and he pulled a dictionary from his rib.

She was awed by his mystery. His head, which was not bigger or smaller than other heads, was full of this...while others it seemed were full of that.

---ellyn maybe

THE EXTENSIVE TRAVELER

For over three years he travelled the world, seeking out humanity's legacy of culture and art. This was his sole devotion, as he traversed the planet far and wide to corners both famous and virtually unknown: to recognize, appreciate and become inspired by the mass of human creation. But although his travels did provide profound inspiration and spiritual enrichment, on his return, the traveler was overcome with plaintive regret.

How could this be? His close friends asked him. After all, he had been privileged to have dedicated to encounter the mass of human artistic accomplishment. Yes, it was true that some works had deteriorated, and others had long ago been destroyed, but in total humanity's treasure was quite remarkable.

It wasn't what was lost that bothered the traveler. Indeed, just knowing about the works that had deteriorated or disappeared was also an inspiration. What bothered the traveler was not the past at all, it was another regret entirely.

I have come to realize that despite all our failings, human potential remains vast and almost unlimited. With humanity destined to thrive for many hundreds of thousands of years more, my regret is for all the works yet to come, the art not yet imagined. None of us, not even I, the extensive traveler will have the privilege to encounter the art that has yet to come.

---pj swift

TRAIN

It's like when a train is making a stop at a city
that's never had a train before.
Sometimes you ride with the baggage.

It's like dreaming night after night of *An American in Paris* and not knowing
if you are Gene Kelly, George Gershwin, Leslie Caron, Nina Foch or
Oscar Levant. Or a medley no one will ever score.

It's like being made of apples and finding you're forbidden.

It's like the episode of *Twilight Zone* where the bandages are removed and
you're still appalling.

It's like finding the perfect Mont Blanc pen and as soon as you put it in
your pocket, the world changes to invisible ink.

It's like someone said come out of the cave decorated with rare L.P.'s and
canaries who rebel against the coal miner's broken throat -- you feel the
avalanche in the bones of the land itching like the first day of junior high.

It's like someone yodeled to you and when you yodeled back, they set fire
to your Nelson Eddy and Jeanette McDonald records.

It's like wearing 3D glasses and saying, "let's be silly together" and the
other person saying "G-d, you're ugly."

I trusted you.
I've worn glasses since I was two.

---ellyn maybe

TWO TRAINS RUNNING

Two trains running
on two parallel tracks
Two trains passing
with two opposite tacks

A view from the window
evokes a look into a mirror
as each opposite train
quickly grows nearer

an approaching traveler is watching
from the same seat as mine
his window a frame
into a warped passage of time

gone in a rumble,
what did he see?
something totally different?
or precisely the same as me?

What is he sensing
as he enters the terrains I have passed?
been there done that?
or aching nostalgia
for times he has lost?

Maybe there's wonder,
sensations to breach
Maybe anticipation
for the destinations he'll reach

Maybe we're disparate and share only what every soul thinks:
that we're special, distinctive and completely unique

---pj swift

WHIFF OF WONDER

There's such a pain in the world.
Like we all stepped on a thumbtack at the same time.
And we can either take a step forward or a step back.
But there is something in the collective paw of the world.
Holding us up.
For some it's music, for some it's a rainbow.
For some it's nature, for some it's love.
The world must contain wonder when it feels all the breath and wishes
contained.
Even a whiff of wonder at the right moment in time
Can do wonders.
Living in the world.

---ellyn maybe

PERENNIAL

It's a wholly expected miracle
Flowers bloom on regular occasion
Sometimes more, sometimes less
blossoming is inevitable
and yes, those buds can be snapped
or, trampled upon
But always something will bloom
somewhere, somehow, again

Do poems flow from the same spring?
Unstoppable, perennial, always blossoming
infinitely unique
invariably miraculous
providing scent and color
and asserting life

---pj swift

ETERNAL EPONINE

If you've seen Les Mis, you know what I mean.
If you've been to high school, you also know.
Life is a musical on the very best days.
Life is a musical on the very worse days.
Musicals walk our emotions on the slippery emotional slope of childhood;
Weirdness, Defiance, Acceptance and the Wisdom to know you are
the difference.
Life is a theatrical terrain and we break the 4th wall carrying a curtain and a
ghost light.
Breakfast is full on pancake makeup.
Lunch is props from The Apple Orchard.
My Dinner is with Andre.
I'm Eternal Eponine,
The most reliable narrator I've ever seen.

---ellyn maybe

POETRY HOUSE

People started to flow into the modest, nondescript house near the corner of the street. Quickly, the ground floor was full of revelers who began to recite lines of verse one by one. As they each took turns reciting their lines, their recitation soon became unified. Altogether, those who had gathered, young and old alike, from different walks of life were chanting as one.

Outside, the cramped house began to pulse, breathing with the rhythmic lines of poetry that the revelers all lived and shared. The windows steamed, and wisps rose from the chimney. The color of the house lightly fluctuated from gray to soft pastels.

And the poem finished. The revelers held a solemn breath, and then each took their leave. The tiny house was again empty, nested in peaceful anonymity near the corner of the street.

---pj swift

PEOPLE

There are people who hold an abridged tablet of the Ten Commandments
in the space between their teeth and jaw.

There are people who come into a room with stardust on their breath like a
lullaby of backward halitosis.

There are people who hold the planets together by clicking their
Achilles' heels three times.

There are people who skywrite without an airplane, without a net.

There are people who twirl a room like a rodeo for the sheepish.

There are people who have bowling parties in their pajamas while the rest
of the world seems like a pin waiting for an angel to step out onto the
dance floor.

There are people who seem to have eyeball upon eyeball like gumballs in
an arcade of vision.

There are people who walk into a room, a thermometer preceding them.

There are people who wear their weather like perfume.

There are people who know the cuckoo is the state bird of most
states of mind.

There are people who went to the same high school and spent each recess
in the lost and found room uttering their phonetic name.

There are people who will have conversations deep as deathbed
soliloquies and never speak again.

There are people who make whatever street they're on
Telegraph Avenue 1964.

There are people who write a shopping list in hieroglyphics.

There are people who look up at the sun 8000 times a day and
lack an eclipse.

There are people who drag questions from the tongue like photos one
second before the crisp of a fire.

There are people who ask nothing, and your heart sits like a blank check in
    a bookstore that sells only elegy.

There are people with a little past behind their ears.

There are people with a newscast on their eyebrows.

There are people no matter how many apples they held,
    teachers resented them.

There are people who ring many doorbells, but won't let themselves in.

There are people who light candles half the week and
    swallow swords the rest.

There are people who memorize the footprints made by the snow.

There are people who dine on shivers.

There are people who chew on icicles all year round.

There are people who pray with the nostalgia of baseball.

There are people who laugh at life openmouthed like a kiss.

---ellyn maybe

PIECE 2/420 (THE "EVERYONE NEEDS" LYRIC)

Everyone needs a mentor
Everyone needs a mom
Everyone needs their heart to flutter
Everyone needs to feel a song

Everyone needs to linger
Everyone needs some time alone
Everyone needs adventure
Everyone needs to ride along

Everyone needs a melody to make their feelings sing
Everyone needs to look around and take in everything

Everyone needs and everyone wants
Everyone thinks they missed their chance

Everyone believes that nobody cares
but reaching out is what nobody dares

Everyone needs a mentor
Everyone needs a mom

Everyone needs a melody, to make their feelings sing
Everyone needs a blessing and feel with everything

Everyone is everyone and no one should be denied
Everyone is never no one, no one should have to hide

Everyone is everyone, every every everyone
every every everyone

---pj swift

MYSTIC BOXING COMMISSION ®

For Extraordinary Books,

Visit the MBC Website at:

www.SparringArtists.com

Coming soon to MBC!